Hi everyone we will provide you with detailed instructions you step by step how to build a professional looking website. Now, what's great about this is that you don't have to be a web developer or know how to code in order to be able to build a professional looking website in a very quick amount of time. But this is going to be a condensed, most important part of building a website to get you from where you are now without a site to getting you to a fully built out site as fast as possible. So let's get started here.

Hosting

I will be using a website called Hostgator, which is a hosting service that you need to host your website on and you certainly don't have to use Hostgator but it is the one that we're gonna be using. So if you want to follow along, And you can start for as low as $2 and 75 cents per month, if you want to go through and kind of sort through them and find the one that might be the best fit for you.

And then we're going to see three different options for hosting our website. So at the lowest tier, which we can get for as low as $2 and 75 cents per month. And then we also have two higher Plans as well. I'll just be using the cheapest option here, plan for $2 and 75 cents per month. But you probably will notice that there will be some upsells along the way. And this is where we're at right now, which is going through the process of choosing our domain, choosing our hosting plan, signing up with certain information that we need, and then deciding on how long of a plan we're looking for.

So for choosing a domain here, as I'm highlighting up top here, you can see hostgator.com that is the domain that we are on right now. Sometimes you'll see things like Amazon.com, that's a domain so you need to find your domain name. You already own one, you can just click over here. But if you need to register a new one, we can just type in here and let's find a domain. Let's say for this to be kylieart.com is going to be our domain that we will use for this new website that we're creating. So see if it's available, it looks like it is available as a primary domain. So that's pretty great to see. And then we also look like they're running a special offer at the moment, which is giving us that free one year domain registration on select annual plans.

So we are getting a nice discount there, we're getting that free domain for a year. Hostgator runs a number of different promotions depending on the time in the year at the moment. So you know, maybe you'll see something different, maybe you won't see this free domain for the first year, depending on the time but it might be running some other promos as well.

Privacy Protection

What the heck is up with all the emails you've been getting with privacy policy updates and Terms of Service updates from like every company you've ever signed up with an account with? Well, we're going to say why this is happening, how it's going to impact you and some actual changes you're going to see in the future.

And the answer is that this is all because of a new law that went into effect just recently, and it is called the GDP our general data protection regulation, which specifically affects the European Union. And while this law was actually passed, like two years ago, in 2016, it only just went into effect this Friday, the 25th. And a lot of companies were required to update their privacy policies. And of course, even though they had two years to do it, they kind of waited till the last minute to do it. So you're getting all these flooded emails at once.

And while that may seem kind of boring, there is actually a lot more to it that you will probably be interested in. So let me explain a little bit more in detail why this is important. The whole idea is to offer better privacy protection for users and prevent things like unnecessary data collection, that sort of thing. And while this technically only applies to people in the European Union, a lot of these companies are just updating their entire privacy policy. So it applies to everyone, including those in the United States and elsewhere. So while it may seem like these emails are annoying, you can kind of think of every email you receive as you slapping those companies across the face, because they definitely would rather not want to update these privacy policies, because they are literally getting less data about you. And it's better for us, not so great for them, which is better in my opinion.

Now, the entire text of this regulation is quite long. It's like 99 articles or sections, and most of them do describe individual powers that the user will get from now on. So here's a couple random examples. One of them is article 16, which basically says that if a company or data processor has information about you, that is incorrect, You can force them to fix it and get the updated information by telling them presumably, or if they have incomplete information about you, you can also force them to add that information to complete it.

Article 17 is a popular one, you may have actually heard of this before. And it is the right to be forgotten. And this basically says that if a company no longer needs your information for the purpose it was originally collected, they have to delete that information, they can't just hold on to it for no reason. And if you withdraw consent to have your data, and they don't have any legal authority or reason to keep that data longer than again, they have to remove that data if you tell them to and also a part of that is a requirement that they have to get your consent to collect any information about you.

But you gotta be careful because a lot of these companies are definitely going to be really sneaky. You know, they might put it in the terms of service that you're used to just automatically clicking agree and they'll put it all the way at the bottom or maybe it'll be like a pop up on the site that says oh, you agree with To collect cookies, and you're just again used to just clicking it. So you might want to pay attention to that from now on.

Another important requirement is that anytime there is a data breach we've seen a lot of these and companies kind of held back on telling users if they are required within 72 hours of finding out about a data breach to notify affected users, and a certain regulatory body in the EU. So hopefully, from now on, if there's any breaches, you'll now find out about it right away instead of these companies waiting like months or years for telling anyone. And then the final example we can mention here is that if a company does collect information about you, they are required to have data portability, which means that they're required to allow you to download that data and see what actual information they have collected about you.

So you can either download it yourself or move it to other services, and that sort of thing. So no longer can they just hoard all this information and not tell you anything about it. Now you may be thinking, well, what's to stop these companies from doing it anyway, I mean, a lot of times they just do it and just eat the fine but it's actually pretty significant penalties, for example, they can be fined up to $20 million, or 4% of the company's global revenue, whichever is greater for that year. So that's pretty insane if you think about it, not just 4% profit 4% revenue.

So if a company violates the GDPR, then if they have a very low profit margin, then they could very well be taking a huge hit, and it's $20 million, or that 4%, whichever is greater. So it's definitely going to affect them. So this should hopefully make it so companies really have no choice. They're going to have to follow the law. God forbid they do that you know what I mean? So why don't I give you a few quick real examples. So you can see this in action. So one example is Twitter. If you go into the settings, there's a new tab called your Twitter data.

And then if you go down, there's a section called interests and adds data. And this will actually tell you a lot of information you couldn't have before. For example, which advertisers have your contact info and have been using that to advertise to you. And then you can also request that entire list of advertisers. It'll also tell you which interests Twitter has inferred or guests that you have based on your tweet activity and see all those interests it thinks you have, and then remove that and stuff. So it's a really good idea to take a look at that at least. And just to see what information, Twitter or other websites have either gathered from you or kind of calculated about you. And it might be surprising.

And then another example would be Facebook, you can go to the settings and add settings. Again, this will show you which interests you have based on what Facebook has calculated, or pages you've interacted with or whatever. I'm not sure how they did that. And there's another one for advertisers. And it's a good way to see which advertisers used your email or contact information to start advertising you again, this is a good way to see Which advertisers actually had your contact information before and plug that into Facebook.

And a lot of these, I don't know how they got my contact information. Some of these I've literally never heard of, like a lot of music artists. And I imagine what happened is you signed up for some website, and then they made you agree to be able to share it with third parties. And now before you know it, there's a ton of other services and companies and websites that now have your email address, and then you end up on a ton of different advertising lists. So again, you can go in there and remove yourself from those advertising lists, although presumably you can't take away your contact information. If they already have it. You'd have to go specifically to them but it's still good to see and pretty crazy how many of these companies had your information you never even knew about it.

So that's really basically the lowdown on the whole thing and why you're getting these emails and actually recommend that you do read them. If it's a website that at least is important to you. You use a lot. Apparently these regulations and privacy policy updates are required to be in plain English, so it's easy to understand. So they can't just hide behind a bunch of legal jargon so you don't understand it. So these emails again, might say, well, oh, by continuing to use our service, you agree to it. So it's important to actually read these emails at least.

Now we want to look right here at domain privacy. Domain privacy protection is very important in my personal opinion, although I think many people will agree with that. Let's go down here. And let's look at the hosting plans that are available. So as I said earlier, we're going to go have a basic Plan, right, this is the cheapest option. If you want to just kind of go out right away and try to fire up a big website, you can go with the higher plan. we'll keep it simple, go to the basic plan.

And you know what, let's say we just go for 12 months, actually, instead of the 36 months, it's going to be cheaper upfront, although per month, when you average it out over the years, it's going to be more expensive to go with a shorter period of time, like the 12 month, but maybe I don't want to sink tons of money into it right away. I just want to sync maybe enough for the website for one year instead of three years. So let's go with that for this and then we're just gonna have to enter in Our username and our security pin that we're going to create. So once I did that, then we're going to enter in our billing information. I think this is pretty straightforward.

Professional Email

It's almost impossible to do business these days without an email address. While it can be tempting to try and save funds by using one of the many free email options available, when you're running a business it's important to have a professional email address, and it will be well worth the dollars you spend. This is why.

Maintaining a professional image

In business, maintaining a professional image is important for keeping your customers' trust and appearing credible online. When potential or existing customers contact you with questions, or if you reach out to them or to other businesses, using an address like michael@amazon.com.uk definitely looks more professional than michael455564@gmail.com. Routing your email through your business's domain name shows that your business is well-established and genuine, and is likely to make customers feel more comfortable dealing with you.

Clear link to your website

A professional email address using your domain name makes it easy for customers to look up your company and your website for more information. This also contributes heavily to reassuring them that you are a legitimate and established business, and engenders trust. It's a great marketing asset too – any email you send, or any time you leave your contact details with someone, you're also giving them an easy link to your website.

Reduce the risk of being marked as spam

Exactly because anyone can sign up for a free email address quickly and easily, they are frequently used by spammers, and as a result are often viewed with suspicion – this is why having a professional email address connected to your own domain is such a trust marker. Some spam and malware filters will automatically disable, or reroute to Junk Mail folders, emails from providers like Hotmail, for example. A professional email address reduces the risk of your business emails bouncing or being sent straight to the trash can.

Organise your emails by purpose

Organising your incoming mail by assigning particular email addresses to departments or purposes – for example accounts@companyname.com, info@companyname.com – not only helps you from the perspective of managing your workload, but adds credibility to your business by further reinforcing that you are an established presence.

Collaborate with your team

Professional email addresses powered by solutions like Office365, G suite typically come bundled with other features like shared calendars which make collaborating with your colleagues much easier. You can send and manage meeting requests, view your workmates' calendars and check their availability, and even hold virtual meetings and work on shared documents at the same time using these kinds of tools.

Now we're getting down here to section number five, which is entering in a coupon code. But if you enter it, you'll notice that you'll end up saving about $60. For that, so you know, it's kind of a win win. Sometimes Hostgator will give us a commission when we get people to sign up for it. A lot of different companies will try to get us to do this. But we genuinely do like a hostgator. And you know, it is a win win for everyone.

So if you want to enter the code, you certainly can but don't feel pressured to in any way. So once we've entered all of that information, we'll see that our total cost comes out to about $122. But you know what, let's say we want to make this cheaper. Let's actually get rid of this SSL certificate and see how low that price is going to be. And now we're just getting about $80 for a 12 month plan for a website. So this is what this is about $6 and 67 cents per month. I don't know if they did that math right in my head, but I'm pretty sure I did. So for $6 and 67 cents per month.

Privacy Policy

I'll be discussing website policies. Website policies are mainly the policies that are governing the users and you as a company or an entity owning and providing a platform for anybody across the globe. These website policies mainly consist of the terms and conditions that are put forth while accessing the platform or the use of any products or services through your platform. website policies are of various types, Terms of Service, privacy policy, content policy, Cookie policy, display policy, so on and so forth. I'll be focusing upon two major policies.

They are the terms of service and privacy policy Terms of Service. Service is mainly the conditions set forth on your platform for the users accessing your platform or availing any services or purchasing any products through your platform. Terms of Service is mainly for the purpose of the users to identify the product, their availability, their usage, and so on and so forth. Privacy Policy, on the other hand, is the governance of the personal information provided by the users on the platform, what you do with it and what you do not do with the Privacy Information provided by the users on the platform.

This information can ideally be your photo name, date of birth, age, address, mobile number, personal details, so on and so forth. And it is very essential for any platform till is down the privacy policy for the only reason being that the Users are safe when they are providing the information on your platform. With the current laws and current regulations in place in India, as per the Information Technology Act of 2000 the terms of service and privacy policy are two essential documents that have to be listed on your platform in order for your platform to be listed for public use. A failure of which will result in takedown of your platform.

So just click this box once you obviously read their terms of service and the cancellation policy and the privacy policy, I would suggest reading that over. Once you do that, then you can just click on checkout now. So let me do that. And then let's go into the important part of this which is actually building the website here.

Alright, so here we are on the next page that they throw us into and the payment has been completed. And it's gonna take a little bit of time to set up your account. So don't worry if this takes more than a few minutes. Sometimes I've seen this take a little bit longer up to 30 minutes. So look They're building our Hostgator account at the moment, if you want to take a break, now you know you go get a cup of coffee or something, come back to it. And then you're going to get ready to build out your site. Now here we are loaded actually pretty quickly.

And now we are on the Hostgator dashboard here. So what we're actually going to do is we're going to end up clicking over on marketplace over on the left, but definitely get familiar with the dashboard here. So let's actually just click on View your dashboard here. And this is our dashboard, we're going to see different options here. You know, we can add the SSL certificate if necessary.

Wordpress Installing

But let's click up here on the marketplace because now we're going to actually install WordPress, which is going to be how we're going to build our site. WordPress is totally free. Once you already paid for Hostgator you're not gonna have to worry about paying for WordPress, it's open source. And so we're just gonna go through this process here, click on site builder and CMS. And then from here, we're going to click on WordPress, which as you can see, like I said, is free. Okay, so now that we're at this point, this is where we are going to be installing WordPress.

So WordPress is by far far the best option for building a website in my opinion, there's plenty of other ways to do it as well. But if you're using Hostgator, I think it really matches well with something like WordPress. So let's just click on Kylieart website here, right? Now let's go and click on Next. Okay, so now that we've done that, we're going to just fill in some information here, right, so our blog title, the admin user, first name, last name, admin email, in this situation here, this is actually where we are creating our WordPress account. So make sure that you do remember this information, it's going to be pretty important to do this.

Let's get started

First, create your WordPress.com account.

Your email address

Choose a username

Choose a password

By creating an account, you agree to our Terms of Service.

Create your account

Or create an account using:

G Continue with Google

🍎 Continue with Apple

If you continue with Google or Apple and don't already have a WordPress.com account, you are creating an account and you agree to our Terms of Service.

Log in to create a site for your existing account.

Let's say the blog title is Kylieart website admin user. It's going to be let's just say Kylie, first name Kylie, and last name Jenner. And then we're going to add my email as well. And then we're going to click on Install. Make sure you read their terms of service as well of course, which is an important step in the process here and then we're going to click on install WordPress. Okay, so let's just do this now. Okay, and then this is actually Gonna take you a little bit of time as well. So don't worry, of course, if it takes you a little bit longer.

But now it looks like it came up relatively quickly. I actually skipped for about two minutes here to wait for it to load, you're going to see your username and your password, these are going to be important. And these are your installation details, make sure that you write these down, maybe just take a picture of it or something. You can change these later. But this is how you're actually going to be able to log into WordPress.

So you have your username, which is Kylieart, which is my username, and then they gave me these big, long passwords that I'm going to save and you'll copy and paste it and then I will go to login. Now we can just click on login if we want to. But let me actually just copy this here and just copy to my clipboard and then I'm going to click on login. This takes us to our WordPress login here. Okay, so enter the information that they just gave you on the previous page. So my username is Kylieart. Oh, I'll paste my password here. Right. Okay, so this part seems to be pretty straight forward. And then you know what, let's just have it remember me for now, and then I'll click on login Alright, so no, I don't want them to save that, email does look correct for now of course, you can go back and you can change all of this information later if you'd like to. But this is our WordPress dashboard. Something to keep in mind is that if you want to get to your WordPress dashboard and you don't want to go through Hostgator every time, you can go up here, and if you just type in your domain, and then forward slash WP dash admin, just how it looks here.

This is going to take you to your WordPress login, right so if you're trying to get back to this page over here right now, just type in your domain and then the forward slash WP dash admin to get to that. Okay, so let me just exit out of some of the things here that are cluttering up my WordPress dashboard. I just don't like having all this clutter here. And then we can see two here. It says that our site is currently displaying a coming soon page.

So once you're ready to launch your site, we can click here so let me click here. And automatically now our site is live which means that if we go to Kylieart.com It's going to be our website. So let me actually minimize this. I already went to it to just kind of check up on it. But yeah, if we click Refresh here, this is our website, right? Our website is live on the internet. And you can go to it right now, we go to Kylieart.com, and this is our website, and doesn't look very good, right? I mean, honestly, it looks terrible. But we have to start somewhere, right. So it's pretty cool. I mean, this is a live website, on the internet that anybody can access and you've already gotten this far. There's but there's a couple things that I think are really important if you want to make this look like a very professional website, in a relatively short period of time. So what I'm going to do now is we're actually going to go over and we are going to click on appearance.

Themes

Okay, so let's then click on themes, and then we'll add a new theme right here. Okay, and from here, we can browse a number of themes that are available on WordPress that are free themes to use. So let me just kind of scroll through here. You know, I like Lenovo. I've used it before, we can go through and we can find ones that maybe we think would be a nice theme. So let's actually just search for one that I've used quite often, which is Astro.

Astro is one of the most popular WordPress themes. It is free, they have a pro version, but it is free.

So let me click on Install. And once it installs, then we're gonna have to actually click activate. And it should be pretty quick. So let's click Activate now. Okay, and now it has been activated, which means that actually, let's go back and let's visit our site and let's see how it's looking. So minimize this. Go back to Kylieart.com, let's hit the refresh button and see how it looks. We're gonna be doing this quite a bit just to kind of see our progress. And look how it changed right there. Right, so this is the Astra theme, it's already starting to look a little bit better.

I mean, it still doesn't look like a very good website. But we're starting to get there, right? This is the Astra theme. So let's go back here. And we'll start to touch up this website a little bit more. So now what I think what we're going to do is let's actually go and let's start to add some different pages here. If you want So, look, so right here, we just have the sample page, right, but let's add some more, let's add maybe a blog or a contact or something else along here, up at the top, so that we can kind of create this navigation center for our website.

Alright, so let's go back and click on pages. Okay, so when we click on pages, and we're going to see a couple of pages that have already been created for us with hostgator. It looks like they already like installed WP forms, which you know, for now, I don't want that I do find it to be a decent plugin, but for now, I'm just gonna trash it. And then sample pages as well. I'm gonna trash that one too. I just don't want that right now to clutter up my WordPress dashboard.

The Privacy Policy, that is an important step in most websites, but we're not going to touch on that right now. You can fill that out. so let's go up and let's hover over new and then let's click on the page.

Okay, so we're creating a new page. And the first one, I think we're gonna need a homepage, we're gonna need a blog, we're gonna need a contact page. Let's wait for this to load here. And then we'll start creating some of these pages. Okay, so let's x out of this right here. Just trying to Get through some navigation. And for this, you know, let's just make a blog page, right? Because maybe Kylieart website is gonna be primarily a blog, click publish, click Publish again, it's going to update it.

Okay, and now let's go back, let's click on the WordPress logo here, we're gonna go back and then we're going to add another page here. So click Add New. And now, let's add another one. Okay, so let's say products, is going to be one of our other pages, click publish, Again, it's going to update, click back on the WordPress logo, rinse and repeat, right and maybe do this for as many new pages as you want to create for that navigation bar up top.

If you're creating a post that can be different, I'll show you how to do that as well. If you're creating blog posts, that's not gonna be a page. So for this, we'll say contact is going to be a pretty important straightforward page here. So we'll publish that. And then we'll go back here.

So I think that's probably good. We probably should add a homepage as well. But let's just kind of brush over that right now. Okay, so now let's check on this website again, click Refresh. And now we can see a boom in the upper right corner, we have blog contact and products. So we're getting some, right I mean, the Kylie website still looks terrible.

Plugins

So now, what I want to do here is we're actually going to go plugins here. And we're going to add a new plugin, but let's just click on plugins to see what we have for now. But let's go up here. Let's click Add New. And these are going to be some pretty important plugins.

The first one is going to be Elementor. This is going to be essentially it makes WordPress like a drag and drop feature for building your website. So like if you've seen Squarespace or Wix, it reminds me very much of the Elementor page builder, it is free. It does have a free version, but it also has a pro version. I mean, you can see here five plus million active installations.

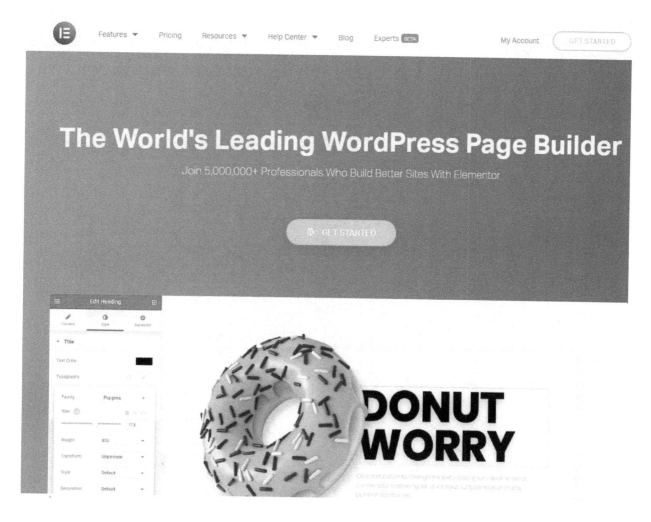

It's one of the most popular page builders you can use Elementor or you can use Divi, both I find to be very great. And the good thing about Elementor is that they have that free version. So that is a pretty good benefit there, right? So we're going to install it. And then we have to go and click on activate. To get this Elementor page builder, this is probably the most important plugin.

Although there will be some other plugins that I do want to show you as well, they're gonna throw us into this little thing about Welcome to Elementor. Also just x out of that for now. And here we are, let's go to pages actually. And I just want to do one more thing before we jump the gun here. And that's going to be actually adding a homepage, which is going to be pretty important. I actually just forgot to do that. So we're going to add a home page, because when you start building out our homepage for the website to make it look beautiful right. So let's view the page here. Just check up on a sales looking Okay, so here's the homepage, right.

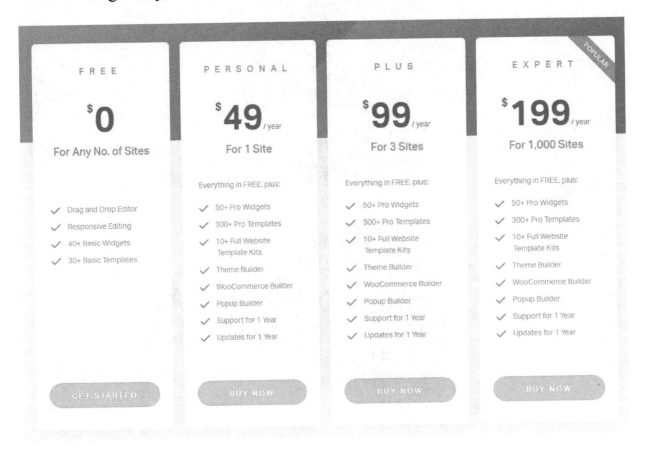

These are out of order up in the upper right, but we'll fix that at some point. Let's go up here and click Customize though because I want to change the layout here. I don't like this sidebar. So let's get rid of that sidebar, right so I clicked up on Customize and just have to wait for it to load from Second. And now let's say that I don't like that sidebar, right, I can click on the sidebar here. So let me click on here.

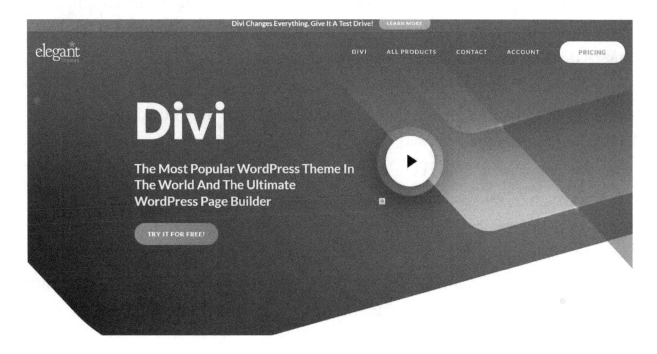

And let's, we can decide if we want no sidebar, left sidebar, right sidebar, let's say no, no sidebar, right? I don't want a sidebar, and click Publish. And there we go. Right. So now we don't have a sidebar. And we can start to mess around with different things as well, you know, I would suggest going through this and just kind of looking at each one of these, right, so let's go down to homepage settings.

And we can alter this. So our homepage displays, we want to be a static page, instead of just our latest posts. So we're gonna click a static page. So we want our homepage to display right? This is pretty important. And then we want our post page to probably display our blog. So let's click down here on posts, and let's display our blog for the post page. And for the homepage, we have home.

This is a pretty important step that some people get caught up on and they don't understand how to organize their website. Okay, so now that we've done this, I do suggest like I said, just kind of going through and learning about these different things, but down here, you can see these three different options right here, this tablet here is mobile, right? So I've clicked on the little phone icon down there. This is what your site looks like on mobile. Okay, so you can check that out. Well, a lot of websites are visited on phones these days. I know some websites have more traffic from phones and they have from websites or from desktop, but just kind of go through this and work through each one of these right? Look at the header, look at global homepage settings, widgets, menus, footer, right, go through and just sort of learn your way around this so that you can find out, you know, the best settings for yourself for your website.

Okay, so now that we've done that, let's actually start to build out this homepage because it looks pretty blank right now. So let's go back to the dashboard here. Okay, let's start to build a page here. Okay, so we hover over pages. Let's actually just click on it here. And here are our current pages at the moment. So let's click on Home here, let's let's open up the homepage so that we can start building that out. So let's click on Edit.

And from here, you can certainly edit your page, just like on WordPress like this, like I can just start typing and you'll see this pop up, but it's going to look very newspapering. So what we want to do to make it look really nice is click on edit with Elementor up here with this blue button. And now it's gonna load Elementor page builder, which is super cool. Like I said, this is like the most important tool that you're gonna find that you're installing for WordPress.

And they have this free version, we're using the free version, so don't feel inclined that you have to upgrade to the pro version, although the pro version, I think is about $50 a year. So it's pretty inexpensive. But from here, we can just drag and drop things right. So let's say that we want to drag and drop a video, right? Let's say we want to drag and we'll just put a video here. So right there, we just added the video, right? It was that simple.

We just literally drag the video over and we can delete it if we want to. That was a pretty large video. We can add different things as well, right? So we can go down here, go through and start to learn your way around Elementor.

Right, so we just added a button here, you can mess around with it and start to learn about it quite a bit to see how you can build your site as best as possible.

But this is gonna be probably the easiest way to build out your website. But you know, while this can be very customizable, if we want to go with a quicker route, right? If we want to go with something that's essentially a template that we can install, which is going to be faster than just using Elementor alone.

I'll show you how to do that. Okay, so let's click up here and let's actually go back to our WordPress dashboard because what we're gonna do now is we're going to install a theme. And this is going to be a free theme that we can get, which is going back to the plugins section here.

Okay, so hover over plugins, let's add a new plug in here. And this plugin that we're going to be adding is called Envato. So Envato also has free versions, you don't have to pay for them, you'll find that most WordPress plugins have like a free version, and they have a paid version. And in a lot of cases, you can still use the free version and get away with it right. So let's let's activate Envato here, and then we'll see it pop up here.

And I might be skipping around a little bit, but let's click over on elements here. Let's click on elements. And let's look at our free template kits that we have. Okay, so from here, these are our free templates that we can install. And we can essentially just fast track our website to make our website look like this very quickly. So we click Install Kit here. Right? We can view the kit and this is what we're looking at. Okay, so let's say, you know, I like these. These look really cool.

So I'm Want to just make this into my homepage. So we'll go back to pages here. And we will go back to edit with Elementor on our homepage. So we're going back to where we were previously when I was showing you how to use Elementor. Right, so we're on a homepage, we're going to build this out. But now we see this green button up here, which is the Envato element symbol. So when you click on that row, we'll see our installed templates, right? So we have this cybersecurity template, and we can click on the View installed kit, right.

And let's say that from here I really like this design home one let's say that I want to insert a template home, so I click on it and it starts to import. It might just take a little bit of time. So once this loads, this is going to essentially be our website is going to look like this and we can just start to edit and modify the wording right so boom, just there like that. Our website looks so much more filled out already. We can click Update.

And actually what I'll do is I'll go back to Kyliaeart.com we'll click Refresh. The live website here, right? So I just clicked refresh here. And now Whoa, our website looks way fancier, with just a couple of clicks of a button. Obviously the wordings are not correct I mean, the wording just looks completely off. This is talking about cyber security of some type.

And we're talking about the Kylie Art website, which is something totally different. But this template allows us to essentially just change words, we can change different ideas, buttons, add pictures, change the background, but it gives us something to work with, which I find to be so useful, especially for beginners. And if you're in sort of a time crunch, or you just don't really want to have to deal with building a website from scratch, we can import these templates and let's say I want to change this instead of whatever that just said.

And let's just say I want to make the title of Kylie, something right. So I can do that super easily by just adding and deleting things from this pre-built template that was free from Envato elements. You can just access it through your website dashboard already, if you'd like to see, we can modify these buttons as well, right? So saying click here, maybe want to say something else, we can add a link as well. So it's really, really useful to have these templates.

Let me just change this up, let's say, learn more, instead of clicking here, you probably do want to change up the templates quite a bit, just so that you're not kind of looking like a copy and paste website that other people might be making. But yeah, this is probably the best way to build a website as fast as possible. And you can essentially rinse and repeat this process for different pages that you have for your website. So if we just clicked over on that little thing right there, look, we can use x out of this, right, we can hover over the x, x out of that maybe we don't want those right, maybe we don't like the section of the template, just x out of that.

And you can see what I'm doing here. We can move this one around, right? We can drag it below, drag it above, super simple though. Drag and drop feature with Elementor is going to be one of the best features with building a WordPress website with a hostgator.

Okay, so start to just get to know this. Like I said earlier, we can save it as a template or save as a draft if we'd like to. We don't wanna make it live right away, we can just do that and be pretty simple to do that, right. But those are the biggest features that are the biggest takeaways from building a website with WordPress using Hostgator, Elementor, Envato elements. Those are the biggest plugins that you can use.

Security Plugins

Every day, thousands of sites get taken over or infected with malware. If you want to make sure yours isn't among them, you're going to need a good WordPress security plugin. We're starting right now. So the largest number of active installs means a better plugin. If people don't like the plugin, they wouldn't have it installed. And then the ratings so if you have high ratings five stars is awesome.

1. WordFence Security

WordFence is another stellar security plugin you can add to your WordPress website. It also comes with both a free and premium version, and its purpose is to ensure excellent website security for its users. This plugin is quite powerful,which wordfence Security has on 2 million plus installs, which is pretty awesome. Having that rating for that many installs. wordfence comes in number one by far. And what it provides in the free version is a web application firewall, which basically shifts out all the bad traffic's only good traffic to your site. It allows you to scan for malware on your site and allows you to scan for file changes on your site. Often when hackers get a new site or hacker bots they try to change the files to do certain things on your site other take over your site display different content for your site send emails from your server. It also allows you to track live traffic so you can see who's live on your site right now. You can even see which traffic has been tagged as possibly bad traffic but possibly not it depends on various things but you can see what wordfence thinks the traffic is so either as good as a bad is it a bot is that a human things like that.

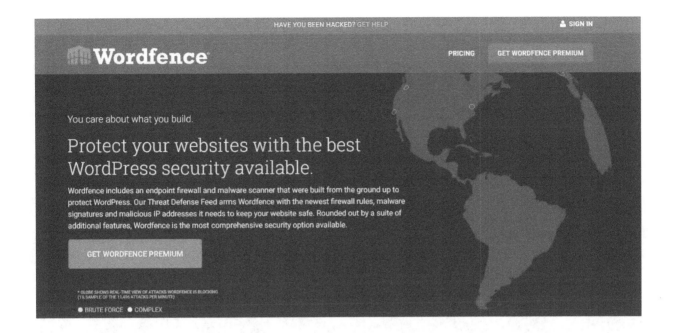

2. I Themes Security

And the next one is I theme security comes in 900,000 active installs four and a half stars and it's a great plugin. And it provides over 25 different ways you can optimize the security on your website. I don't recommend to use them together on the same site because they're both doing basically the same thing. But if you feel you have to make sure that you test it to make sure the site still works, and be sure that if you have something running on wordfence for example, if you're scanning malware, we're using wordfence don't scam malware using iframes. So make sure you're not doing the same exact thing with both plugins. Make sure you have both installed and you're doing different things with each one. Either way I themes is a great plugin.

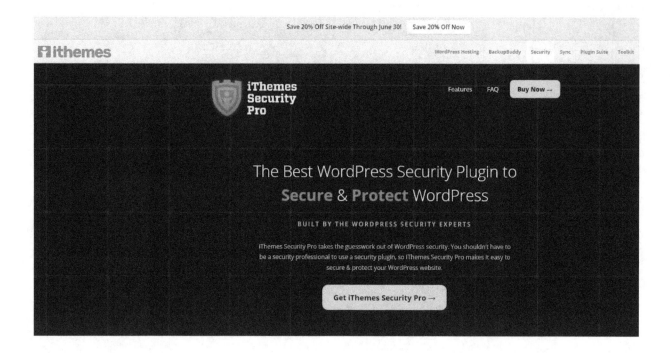

3.All In One – WP Security & Firewall

All in one WP security comes in 700,000 installs five star rating On average, another great plugin you can check out. And again, try not to use all of them, find the one that has the features that you feel you need at this point and install it and try it and see if you like using it.All in one WP security is very popular. And it's a great plugin to check out.

4.Sucuri Security

Sucuri Security is undoubtedly one of the most popular security plugins for WordPress. You can download it for free, but if you plan on using some of its more advanced features, you'll have to sign up for one of Sucuri's paid plans. However, even if you decide to go with the free version only, it should keep your website safe and protected. As soon as you install this plugin, it will automatically run a scan to ensure there are no malware, link injections, infected or suspicious files, etc.

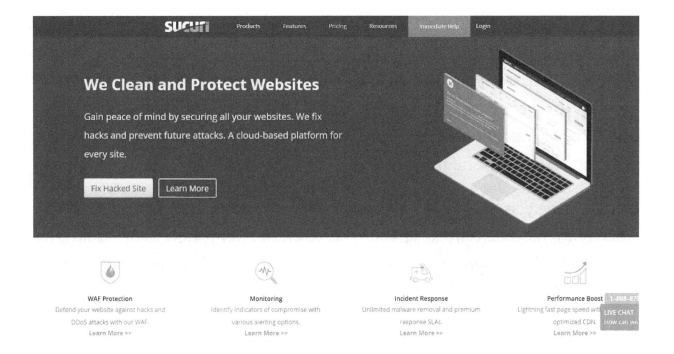

The free version of the plugin takes care of the security activity auditing (it detects things such as failed login attempts), file integrity monitoring (it informs you if someone tries to make any changes to your files), blacklist monitoring (it basically makes sure your website isn't blocked on blacklist engines), and effective security hardening (it removes all vulnerabilities). It also includes security alerts and post-hack security actions (if a security breach occurs, the plugin will provide a list of steps to take). around for security plugins, this is definitely one to check out.

5. Security & Firewall – MalCare Security

The Security & Firewall – MalCare Security plugin stands out from the rest because it not only provides comprehensive protection for your website, but is also fully compliant with GDPR (General Data Protection Regulation).

Only a premium version is available, and there are several pricing packages to choose from.

MalCare comes with an automated malware removal system, a powerful firewall to keep you safe from the latest threats in real time, and it also includes blacklist monitoring. You can run its scanning system daily, which is a tremendously useful thing to do.

In case it detects any kind of changes or malware, it will load your entire content to the MalCare's server, and keep it completely safe from any possible hacks. If you're searching for a paid solution for your website security, MalCare is definitely worth looking into.

Conclusion

To ensure your website remains intact by the bad guys, you need to protect it to the best of your abilities.So really pick one you like, try it out trial, the features found you're comfortable with, maybe even contact their support to see your response to their supporters. Don't run more than one because you might have conflicts. And as a finishing tip, the number one way to keep your site secure is always making sure your plugins, your themes, and your WordPress core files are up to date, because most updates include security patches.

'A information can be obtained
'CGtesting.com
.he USA
.61802070920
.53LV00032B/2179